# Britain
# Since 1948

John Corn

Published by Collins
An imprint of HarperCollins*Publishers*
1 London Bridge Street
London
SE1 9GF

Browse the complete Collins catalogue at
www.collinseducation.com

© HarperCollins*Publishers* Limited 2012
First published in 2006 by Folens Limited, as part of the *Folens Primary History* series.
Previously published as *A Time to Remember: Britain Since 1930*.

10 9 8 7 6 5

ISBN: 978-0-00-746400-5

John Corn asserts his moral right to be identified as the author of this work, in accordance
with the Copyright, Designs and Patents Act, 1988.

British Library Cataloguing in Publication Data
A catalogue record for this publication is available from the British Library.

Acknowledgements
The author and publisher wish to thank the following for permission to use copyright
material:
Allsport/Adrian Murrell, p29 (bottom right)
British Petroleum, p41 (left)
Camera Press, p29
Corbis, pp5, 19, 21, 23, 26 (left, bottom right), 27 (right), 28 (top), 30, 31, 33, 36, 38
(bottom), 47
Environmental Picture Library, pp42 (right) Graham Burns, 45 H. Giradet
Getty Images, p38 (top)
Hulton Deutsch Collection, pp7, 19, 28 (bottom right), 42
IBM United Kingdom Limited, p46
Imagine/Irene Lynch, pp12, 13
International Stock Exchange Photo Library, London, p4
John Corn, pp16, 41 (right)
National Motor Museum, Beaulieu, p37
NRM/Science and Society Picture Library, p32
Photolibrary, p34
Redferns, pp22 David Redfern, 23 (left) Ian Dickson, 23 (middle) Susan Moore, 23 (right)
David Redfern
Retna Pictures Limited, p18 (top)
Rex Features Limited, pp18, 19
Royal Mint, Llantrisant, p4 (top)
Science Museum/Science and Society Picture Library, p26
Syndication International Limited, pp13, 35
Thomson Tour Operations Limited, p33
Tidy Britain Group, p42
Topham, pp6, 8, 9, 40

Every effort has been made to trace copyright holders and to obtain their permission for
the use of copyright material. The author and publisher will gladly receive any information
enabling them to rectify any error or omission in subsequent editions.

Editors: Saskia Gwinn and Joanne Mitchell
Layout artist: Suzanne Ward
Illustrations: Nigel Chilvers, Tony Randell of Tony Randell Illustration
Cover design: Blayney Partnership
Cover image: K. Hackenberg/zefa/CORBIS

Printed and bound by CPI Group (UK) Ltd, Croydon, CR0 4YY

# Contents

When the Second World War ended in 1945, there were still many problems in Europe. Towns and cities all over Europe had been destroyed. Millions of people had been killed. The war had cost a lot of money and many countries were very poor. The Prime Minister of Britain during the war, Winston Churchill, wanted the countries of Europe to join together in a 'United States of Europe'. He hoped this would help the countries to recover from the war and prevent any future wars.

Winston Churchill made a famous speech about Europe in 1946:

*We must build a kind of United States of Europe. Time may be short. At present there is a breathing space, but if we are to form a United States of Europe – or whatever name it may take – then we must begin now.*

*This special fifty pence coin was minted in 1973 to celebrate Britain joining the EEC.*

In 1957, six European countries formed the European Economic Community (EEC). The main aim of the EEC was to allow more business between the countries of Europe. It also allowed people to travel more easily between the countries. Since then other countries have joined, and more have asked to join.

In 1973, the British government, led by Prime Minister Edward Heath, decided that Britain should join the EEC. A special fifty pence coin was minted in Britain to celebrate.

## A new Europe

1. When was the EEC formed?
2. When did Britain join?
3. Who decided that Britain should join?

*The EU headquarters in Brussels, Belgium.*

*The European Parliament at Strasbourg.*

The EU has its own parliament based in Brussels. The European Parliament has members from each country of the EU and passes laws which the member countries have to follow to bring about greater integration and prosperity for all. The Members of the European Parliament (MEPs) are chosen by an election in each country.

There are now 25 countries in the EU and more countries are hoping to join. Some people still like Winston Churchill's idea of a 'United States of Europe', with all the countries joined together under one government. However, not everyone wants this because it might take away the power and identity of their own country as each one would have to obey the laws passed by the other member countries.

## Uniting Europe

The EEC was formed in 1957 for many different reasons. It is growing as more countries join, but not everyone agrees with it.

1. Find out who the first six members of the EEC were?
2. Do you think it is important for the countries of Europe to be joined together in this way? Why?
3. Why is the EEC now called the EU?
4. How do you think the aims of the EU might have changed since 1957?
5. Why do you think some people disagree with the EU?

## Key ideas

election
parliament

**Source A** *Immigrants arriving in Britain in the 1960s.*

In the years after the Second World War there were plenty of jobs in Britain, but not enough people to do them. To fill these jobs, the government asked people in other countries to come to Britain.

Many of the people who came to Britain were from countries once ruled by Britain, such as the West Indies and India. These people had strong links with Britain – for example, many of them held British passports.

People who move to another country to live and work are called immigrants. Immigrants to Britain settled in the large industrial towns of northern England, the West Midlands and in London. They thought they would be welcome in Britain and would have comfortable lives.

|  | 1950s | 1960s | 1970s | 1980s |
|---|---|---|---|---|
| West Indies | 405 000 | 328 000 | 29 000 | 10 000 |
| India | 30 000 | 332 000 | 80 000 | 52 000 |
| Pakistan | 17 000 | 144 000 | 86 000 | 66 000 |
| Bangladesh | — | — | 22 000 | 50 000 |
| East Africa | — | 6 000 | 118 000 | 23 000 |
| Others | 46 000 | 125 000 | 98 000 | 281 000 |
| TOTAL | 498 000 | 935 000 | 433 000 | 482 000 |

During the 1990s, figures show that a total of 1.4 million immigrants arrived in Britain. Tougher legislation is thought to have slowed down figures for the 2000s.

*This chart shows the number of people who moved to Britain between 1950 and 1989.*

| | |
|---|---|
| 1960 | 57 700 |
| 1961 | 115 150 |
| 1962 | 119 770 |
| 1963 | 63 000 |
| 1964 | 3 140 |
| 1965 | 51 200 |

*This chart shows how the Immigration Act of 1962 affected the number of immigrants to Britain.*

**Source B** *An immigrant searching for somewhere to live in 1958.*

New immigrants to Britain were often badly treated. Many of them found it hard to get work and had to take poorly paid jobs. Landlords often refused to rent rooms to them. People who already lived in Britain were often rude or violent to immigrants.

People who make judgements about others based on race, colour of skin or religion are racist. The government tried to ease the problems of racism by passing laws to make it more difficult for people to move to Britain. They also wanted to ensure that immigrants who had already arrived were treated fairly. The Immigration Act of 1962 limited the number of immigrants who could enter Britain each year. However, this did not solve the problems. Racism continued.

Many people moved to Britain before the Act was passed because they thought it would be difficult to get in afterwards.

## Moving to Britain

1. Why did immigrants come to Britain?
2. Why did they settle in industrial areas?
3. Why were there so many immigrants to Britain in the early 1960s?
4. Look at **Source B**. Why has this notice been put in the window?
5. Write a list of words which you think describe the feelings of the people in **Sources A** and **B**.

## Brave new world

Find out more about immigration and racism in Britain.

1. Use an atlas to find which countries immigrants to Britain came from.
2. What happened to the number of immigrants in the 1970s and 1980s? Why?
3. Do you think racism is still a problem in Britain? Give reasons for your answer.

## Key ideas

immigration
racism

Second World War

# 3 The Welfare State

During the Second World War, the government asked Sir William Beveridge and a group of experts to examine living standards in Britain, including poverty, education, employment, health and housing.

In August 1945, the Second World War ended. A new government was elected in Britain, led by the Labour Party. The new government, under the new Prime Minister, Clement Attlee, decided to set up a welfare state in Britain to follow the recommendations of the Beveridge Report.

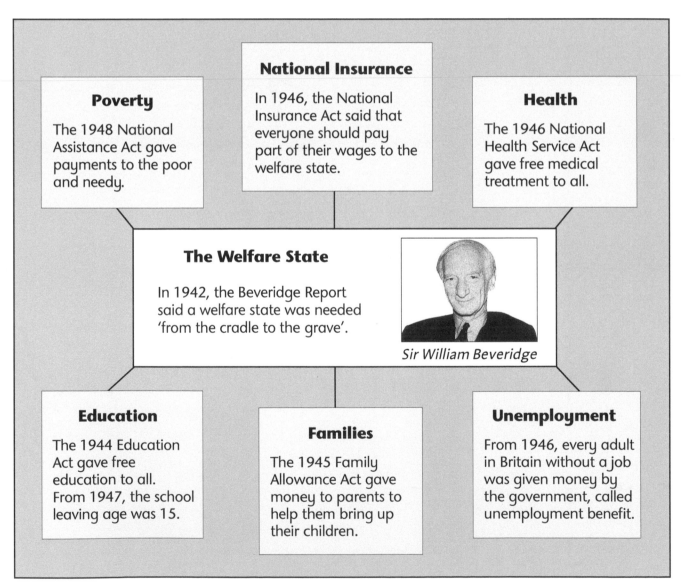

**National Insurance**

In 1946, the National Insurance Act said that everyone should pay part of their wages to the welfare state.

**Poverty**

The 1948 National Assistance Act gave payments to the poor and needy.

**Health**

The 1946 National Health Service Act gave free medical treatment to all.

**The Welfare State**

In 1942, the Beveridge Report said a welfare state was needed 'from the cradle to the grave'.

*Sir William Beveridge*

**Education**

The 1944 Education Act gave free education to all. From 1947, the school leaving age was 15.

**Families**

The 1945 Family Allowance Act gave money to parents to help them bring up their children.

**Unemployment**

From 1946, every adult in Britain without a job was given money by the government, called unemployment benefit.

*This chart shows the main parts of the Welfare State and the main effect of each part.*

One of the most important parts of the Welfare State was the National Health Service (NHS), which gave free medical treatment to everyone. The NHS was very successful in many areas. For example, it helped to reduce the number of children who died from illnesses that could be easily prevented.

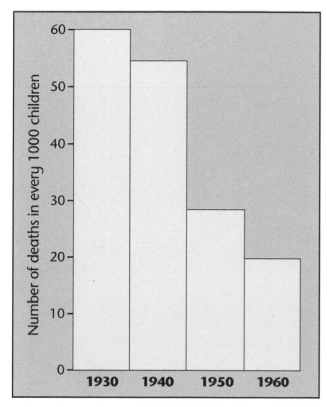

*This chart shows the number of children who died in York between 1930 and 1960.*

During the election in 1950, the Labour Party used posters about the Welfare State to persuade people to vote for them.

**Source A** *A Labour Party election poster, 1950.*

## A new way of life

Find out more about how the Welfare State changed the British way of life in the 1940s.

1. What was the school leaving age before 1948?
2. Write a list of questions to ask an adult aged over 50 about the difference the Welfare State made to their lives.

## Quality of life

1. How did the Family Allowance Act help people?
2. Why was the NHS so important?
3. What might have happened to a poor sick person before 1946?
4. Why do you think the number of child deaths in York went down between 1930 and 1960?
5. Look at **Source A**. Find out produced the poster? Who is it aimed at?

## Key ideas

election          poverty
living standards  Welfare State

**Source B**

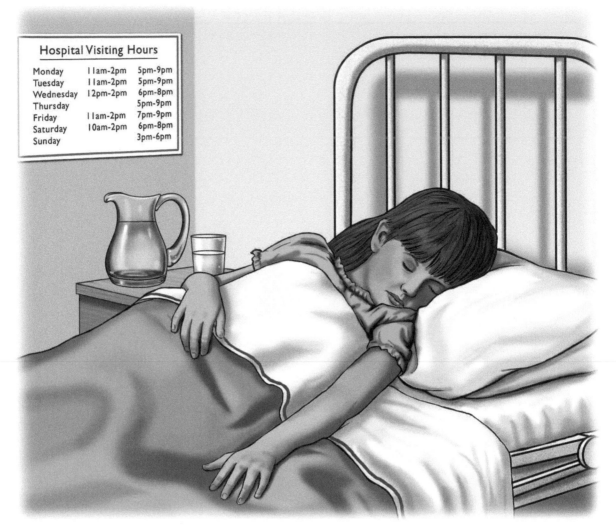

Hospital Visiting Hours

| Monday | 11am-2pm | 5pm-9pm |
| Tuesday | 11am-2pm | 5pm-9pm |
| Wednesday | 12pm-2pm | 6pm-8pm |
| Thursday | | 5pm-9pm |
| Friday | 11am-2pm | 7pm-9pm |
| Saturday | 10am-2pm | 6pm-8pm |
| Sunday | | 3pm-6pm |

**Source C**

## Quality of life

1. Look carefully at **Sources B** and **C**. What does each picture show?
2. In each box, write a way in which the Welfare State could help these people to improve their lives.

## A better way of life

1. Write a list of the ways in which the Welfare State has improved life in Britain.
2. What do you think is the most important part of the Welfare State? Give reasons for your answer.

# 4 Houses and Homes

*Semi-detached houses.*

In the 1950s, many local councils began to clear away bad houses. Previously many families had shared a house with no indoor toilet or bathroom; houses were also close together with no gardens and very little light or fresh air. They began to build estates of houses with gardens. For the first time, ordinary families could buy their own home. New houses were built with electricity, indoor bathrooms and toilets.

However, building new estates did not solve all the problems of bad housing. There were many people living in large towns and cities, but there was not enough land to build houses.

## Quality of life

1. Why did councils need to build new houses?
2. Do you think it was a good idea to build houses with gardens and more space? Why?
3. Why is it important for everyone to have things like electricity, water and a bathroom?

*A large block of flats in London in the 1990s.*

*Many blocks of flats have been demolished to make way for traditional houses.*

In the 1950s and 1960s, many councils decided to build blocks of flats instead of houses. These could be built quickly and cheaply. They took up a small amount of land and gave homes to lots of people.

Many people thought flats like this were the answer to housing problems. People were happy to live somewhere clean and healthy, but soon they had to face new problems. Children who lived in flats high off the ground had nowhere to play. People who lived alone could feel very lonely.

Today, many people still live in high-rise blocks of flats. However, many blocks have been knocked down. Most new homes built today are semi-detached and detached houses on small local developments.

### Key ideas

detached          semi-detached

### A change for the better?

Houses and homes have been built in many shapes and sizes in Britain since 1948.

1. Do you think it was a good idea to build blocks of flats to house lots of people? Why?
2. Why have many of these flats been demolished?
3. In the 1950s and 1960s, 'new towns' were built to move people out of crowded cities. Write a list of these new towns.

## Source A

## Source B

Source D

**Source C**

1970s

In the 1940s, many families attended a church every Sunday. The local church was a very important part of life in towns and villages.

In recent years, going to church has become less popular. Many people think religion is not a very important part of their lives. Only one in every ten people now go to a Christian church every Sunday. Many churches have been sold and are now used as shops, offices or even homes.

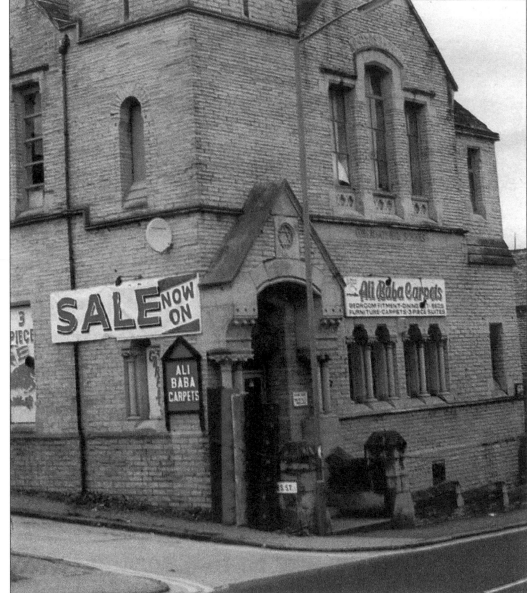

**Source A**

### Going to church

1. What has happened to the church in **Source A**? Why?
2. Why do you think fewer people go to church today? Give two reasons.

Britain is a multi-cultural country. People from many different religions can be found in Britain. Christians and Jews have been in Britain for a very long time, but others such as Muslims, Sikhs and Hindus have come to Britain since the 1940s.

festival                    tradition

*Religious belief can affect every aspect of life, including the way people dress.*

Some of the religions which have become popular in Britain since even before 1948 include Sikhism, Hinduism, Islam and Buddhism. As these different religious groups became popular, they introduced new traditions and festivals. For example, Diwali is a Hindu festival of lights which celebrates the story of Prince Rama and his beautiful wife, Sita. The use of lights at Diwali is similar to the use of lights at the Christian festival of Christmas. For many religions in Britain, light is a symbol of happiness, goodness and rejoicing.

**New religions**

Find out more about the religions that have become popular in Britain in the last half a century.

1. Draw a time line to show which religions first became popular in Britain.
2. Find out about some more religious festivals. Choose one festival and write about it in detail.
3. Draw and complete a chart to show:
   - the main religions in Britain today
   - the main festivals of each religion
   - the holy book of each religion
   - the main symbol of each religion.

# (6) Clothes Line

*Rock 'n' roll, 1955.*

In the 1950s, fashion began to change. The 'Teddy Boy' style was popular, which had knee-length jackets and drainpipe trousers. Women wore long skirts with bright colours and patterns.

*Mini skirts, 1969.*

In the 1960s, 'mini-skirts' were very popular. Denim jeans, shirts and jackets became fashionable.

**Key ideas**

fashion

In the 1980s, fashion became more casual, with sweatshirts, tracksuits and leggings becoming popular.

*Casual wear, 1982.*

In the 1990s, casual clothes were still fashionable, often with certain 'labels' which help to sell the clothes.

*Popular fashions, 1994.*

In the 1970s, bright colours and flared trousers were very popular.

*Flares, 1976.*

*Fashions have evolved since 1948 to these common 2006 examples.*

## Changing fashions

1. Choose one of the fashions from these pages. What does it tell you about life in Britain at the time?
2. What do changes in fashion tell you about the change in British life since 1948?
3. Which fashions have come and gone quickly and which have lasted? Why do you think this is so?
4. Find out more about some of the fashions mentioned, such as Teddy boys or flares.
5. Collect some photographs of the fashions on these pages to make a fashion time line.

# Changing Fashions

Fashion has changed in many ways in Britain since 1948. During the Second World War, clothes were difficult to buy, so people were asked to mend and alter their old clothes.

Today, there are many different fashions and many different materials and fabrics. Wearing fashionable clothes is very important for some people.

## Fashion statements

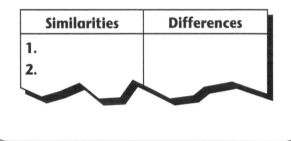

Look carefully at the pictures of fashions in the 1940s and 2000s (**Sources A** and **B**). Copy and complete this chart to show at least two similarities and two differences between each fashion.

| Similarities | Differences |
|---|---|
| 1. | |
| 2. | |

**Source A**  *Ladies' fashions in the 1940s.*

**Fashion sense**

Conduct a survey in your class to find out what fashions are most popular today.

**Source B** *Ladies' fashions in 2000.*

# 7 Pop Music

**Source A**
*Cliff Richard in 1958.*

**Source B** *Bill Hayley and the Comets.*

**Source C** *The Beatles.*

In the 1950s, people began to listen to new kinds of music. Young people began to listen to rock 'n' roll, instead of the slow dance music that their parents had enjoyed.

Young people liked rock 'n' roll because it was loud and fast. New dances such as the jive became popular with rock 'n' roll. In 1955, Bill Hayley and the Comets recorded their song *Rock Around the Clock*. This became the most famous rock 'n' roll song of all time. Other famous singers included Elvis Presley, Chuck Berry and Cliff Richard.

For the first time in the 1950s, records were made cheaper and people could afford to buy them. Cheap record players were also made for the first time. These changes meant that 'pop music' became more popular throughout the 1950s.

In the 1960s, the Beatles became a very popular group. People called them the 'Fab Four' because they were so famous. They were John Lennon, Paul McCartney, George Harrison and Ringo Starr. During the 1960s, they made over 30 hit records. Other pop groups in the 1960s included the Kinks, the Animals and the Rolling Stones. Cliff Richard continued to make records in the 1960s and became a superstar.

**Source D** *The Osmonds.*

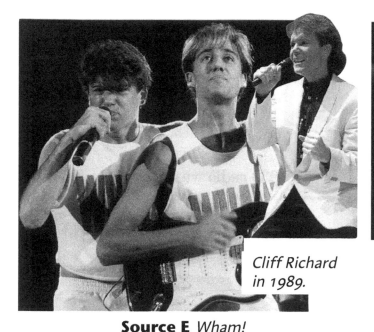

*Cliff Richard in 1989.*

**Source E** *Wham!*

**Source F** *Stereophonics in 2001.*

In the 1970s, rock music was still popular, but people also began to listen to other kinds of music. Styles like punk and reggae became popular.

Pop groups like the Osmonds and the Bay City Rollers attracted groups of teenage fans called 'teenyboppers'. Cliff Richard continued to sell millions of records.

In the 1980s, electronic music and computerised keyboards became popular. Superstars, such as Duran Duran, Madonna and Wham!, sold millions of records.

In the late 1980s, records and tapes were gradually replaced by compact discs, which were much smaller and gave a much clearer sound. Through all these changes, Cliff Richard continued to be popular.

Although CDs are still popular, today new technology means we can download music straight from our home computers.

## Loud and proud

Pop music has changed in many different ways since the 1950s.

1. Collect some photographs of pop groups from 1950 to the 2000s. Make a display showing how pop music has changed.
2. Listen to a pop record from the 1950s, and then one from today. How are they different? Are they the same in any way?
3. Why do you think Cliff Richard has stayed popular since the 1950s?

## Rock around the clock

1. Look at the photographs of pop stars (**Sources A–F**). Write a list of the ways in which pop music changed in each decade.
2. List some of the pop groups that became famous in the 1950s.
3. Why did these groups become popular?
4. How did the style of pop music change during the 1960s?
5. What was different about pop stars in the 1970s?
6. What happened to records and tapes in the 1980s? Why?

## Rock Around the Clock

Pop music first became popular in Britain in the 1950s. Records became cheaper than before, so people could afford to buy them.

Television programmes about pop music also became popular in the 1950s. One of them was called *Juke Box Jury*. Records were played and three people gave them a score between 1 (very bad) and 5 (very good). If the score was good, the record was voted a HIT, but if the score was bad, it was a MISS.

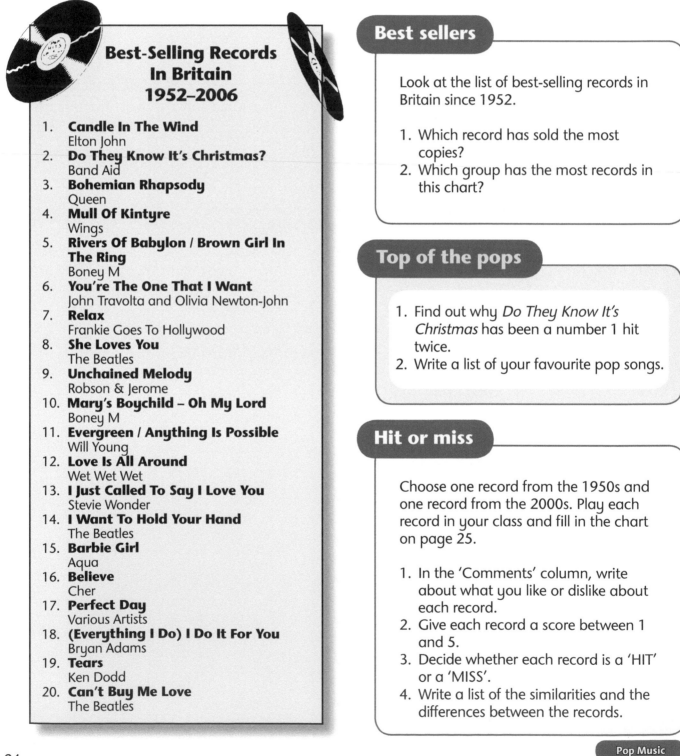

### Best-Selling Records In Britain 1952–2006

1. **Candle In The Wind**
   Elton John
2. **Do They Know It's Christmas?**
   Band Aid
3. **Bohemian Rhapsody**
   Queen
4. **Mull Of Kintyre**
   Wings
5. **Rivers Of Babylon / Brown Girl In The Ring**
   Boney M
6. **You're The One That I Want**
   John Travolta and Olivia Newton-John
7. **Relax**
   Frankie Goes To Hollywood
8. **She Loves You**
   The Beatles
9. **Unchained Melody**
   Robson & Jerome
10. **Mary's Boychild – Oh My Lord**
    Boney M
11. **Evergreen / Anything Is Possible**
    Will Young
12. **Love Is All Around**
    Wet Wet Wet
13. **I Just Called To Say I Love You**
    Stevie Wonder
14. **I Want To Hold Your Hand**
    The Beatles
15. **Barbie Girl**
    Aqua
16. **Believe**
    Cher
17. **Perfect Day**
    Various Artists
18. **(Everything I Do) I Do It For You**
    Bryan Adams
19. **Tears**
    Ken Dodd
20. **Can't Buy Me Love**
    The Beatles

### Best sellers

Look at the list of best-selling records in Britain since 1952.

1. Which record has sold the most copies?
2. Which group has the most records in this chart?

### Top of the pops

1. Find out why *Do They Know It's Christmas* has been a number 1 hit twice.
2. Write a list of your favourite pop songs.

### Hit or miss

Choose one record from the 1950s and one record from the 2000s. Play each record in your class and fill in the chart on page 25.

1. In the 'Comments' column, write about what you like or dislike about each record.
2. Give each record a score between 1 and 5.
3. Decide whether each record is a 'HIT' or a 'MISS'.
4. Write a list of the similarities and the differences between the records.

Pop Music

| Similarities | |
|---|---|
| | |
| **Differences** | |
| | |

| HIT or MISS | Score 1-5 | Comments | Records |
|---|---|---|---|
| | | | |
| | | | |

In the late 1940s and 1950s, television became more popular. By 1949, 344 000 people owned a television set. In 1952, a transmitter was opened in Scotland, and most of the country could receive television.

Even though more and more people began to watch television in the 1940s and 1950s, radio was still popular.

**Source B** *One of the first television sets.*

**Source A** *A radio from the 1940s.*

This was what people saw on the first day of BBC television in 1936:

- 3:00pm – opening speech by the Postmaster General (the man in charge of television)
- 3:15pm – interval
- 3:20pm – news and comedy
- 4:00pm – close

## A look at television and radio

1. Look at the photograph of the radio (**Source A**). How is different from the ones used today?
2. Describe the television in **Source B**. Do you think it would have been easy to watch? Give reasons for your answer.
3. When was the first television broadcast? How long did it last?
4. Look at the list of changes in television since the 1940s. Decide which of these changes was the most important, and then write out the list again, putting the most important at the top and the least important at the bottom.

**An Ipod.**
*In the 2000s music can be downloaded using new technology.*

| 1945 | BBC television began broadcasting again after it closed down during the Second World War. |
| 1955 | Commercial television began broadcasting. |
| 1964 | BBC2 began broadcasting. |
| 1967 | Colour television used for the first time. |
| 1974 | First CEEFAX transmission. |
| 1982 | Channel 4 began broadcasting. |
| 1987 | Satellite television began broadcasting. |

*The main changes in television since the 1940s.*

The BBC also opened two more radio stations in the 1940s. In 1967, Radio 1 was opened, as well as 22 local BBC radio stations. Commercial radio stations began broadcasting in the 1970s.

*Home Cinema equipment for the 2000s.*

### Key ideas

broadcast          commercial

*Inside a modern television studio.*

### TV times

Find out about how television programmes have changed since the 1940s.

1. Make a list of favourite television programmes from the 1940s and 1950s.
2. Make a list of favourite television programmes of today.
3. How have programmes changed in this time?

Sport has always played a very important part in British life. In July 1948, the Olympic Games were held in Britain. It involved nearly 5 000 competitors from 59 countries. Britain was still repairing the damage from the Second World War, so most of the competitors had to stay in army barracks and colleges, unlike the specially built Olympic villages of today.

*England prepare to host the 2012 Olympics. This is a computer-generated image of how a 2012 stadium might look.*

*Roger Bannister ran a mile in less than four minutes in 1954.*

For many years, athletes had tried to run a mile in less than four minutes. On 6th May 1954, Roger Bannister broke the four-minute barrier. His time of 3 minutes 59.4 seconds gave him a place in sporting history.

## Sport in Britain

1. Why was Roger Bannister important?
2. Look at the information on England winning the World Cup. How are the the memories of the two football fans different?
3. What is the footballer in the photograph holding in his hand? Why?

Cricket is another important British sport. Famous cricket players include Fred Truman, Geoffrey Boycott and Denis Compton. One of the most famous cricket matches of recent years was the 'Ashes' match between England and Australia in 2005.

Football is a very popular sport all over Britain. It is the most popular sport on television. One of the most important football events in Britain was England's World Cup victory in July 1966.

*England win the Ashes in 2005.*

England won the World Cup in 1966. This is how one man remembers it:

*I remember seeing it on the television in black and white. It was a brilliant game, England were 2-0 up at half time but it ended up going into extra time. The third England goal bounced off the crossbar and straight into the net. England's fourth came right at the end.*

Another football fan remembers the same match in a different way:

*I'll never forget, it was 30th July 1966 when we won the World Cup, in front of a crowd of 100 000. The teams were drawing one-all at half time and two-all at full time. In extra time Hurst scored his hat-trick. Our fourth goal finished them off.*

## Fun and games

Find out more about sport in Britain since 1948.

1. Collect some information on great moments in sport since 1948. Make a collage for display showing how things have changed.
2. Write a short newspaper story with a headline. Choose one of the sports from these pages, or choose another sport you are interested in.

*England won the World Cup in 1966.*

## Fun and Games

**1.**

**1.**

- _____

- _____

- _____

**2.**

**2.**

- _____

- _____

- _____

**3.**

**3.**

- _____
  _____
- _____
  _____
- _____
  _____

**4.**

**4.**

- _____
  _____
- _____
  _____
- _____
  _____

## Sporting achievements

Look at the list of names in the box.

1. Write the correct names for each picture in each box.
2. Write the correct sport in each box.
3. Write an important sporting event for each of them in each box.

Torvill and Dean

Linford Christie

Kelly Holmes

Andrew Flintoff

In 1936, Billy Butlin decided that people should have a different kind of holiday to those which had been popular, so he invented the holiday camp. Boarding houses and guest houses at the Seaside had been popular ways to spend holidays. This often involved sharing a bathroom with other guests. Guests were also often expected to vacate the boarding house for the whole day, even if it was raining. One of his first holiday camps was opened at Skegness. It had rows of cabins for 1000 campers. The activities included swimming and playing tennis. Many people travelled to the holiday camps by train.

*An advertisement for the Butlin's camp at Clacton-on-Sea.*

*Below is a typical list of activities at a Butlin's camp in the 1940s.*

| | |
|---|---|
| 7:30am | Holy Communion |
| 9:30am | Kiddies' Playtime |
| 10:00am | Keep Fit |
| 10:00am | Parents' Free Hour |
| 10:00am | Bowls |
| 10:30am | Fishing at the Lake |
| 11:00am | All-Day Cricket Match |
| 11:00am | Tombola |
| 11:00am | Dress Rehearsal for the Campers' Concert |
| 11:00am | Swimming and Diving Lessons |
| 11:00am | Dancing Class for Adults |
| 2:00pm | Bowls |
| 2:15pm | Parents' Free Hour |
| 2:30pm | Junior Campers Concert |
| 2:45pm | 'They Walk Alone' – play at the Butlin Theatre |
| 4:00pm | Tea Dance |
| 5:30pm | Presentation of Prizes |
| 7:45pm | Whist Drive |
| 7:45pm | Campers' Concert |
| 8:30pm | Dancing |
| 10:00pm | Penny-On-The-Drum |
| 11:45pm | 'Au Revoir' by the Redcoats |
| Midnight | Goodnight Campers |

## Getting away from it all

1. Do you think that boarding houses were nice places to stay?
2. In what way were holiday camps different?
3. Would people have enjoyed the activities at Butlins in the 1940s? Why?
4. Do you think the advertisement for the Butlin's camp is attractive? Would it work today?
5. Travelling by aeroplane is a popular way of going on holiday. Write a list of places people can go by aeroplane in just a few hours.

*Airports like this one at Gatwick have made holidays abroad much easier and cheaper.*

In the 1960s, people began to spend more money on holidays. Many people no longer wanted holidays in Britain, mainly because of the weather. Package holidays became popular – people arranged holidays through a travel agent, and they paid one price which included the cost of travelling, the hotel and meals. In the 1970s and 1980s, air travel became cheaper. Nowadays it is easy to take a holiday in almost any part of the world, with budget airlines such easyJet and Ryanair making flying a far cheaper experience.

## Different kinds of holiday

Find out more about different kinds of holiday.

1. Write a list of the main differences between a boarding house holiday, a holiday camp and a foreign hotel.
2. Collect postcards from people on holiday and put them on a map. Find out how they travelled and where they stayed.

*A holiday brochure from 1961.*

### Key ideas

package holiday

33

In 1962, the government decided that the railways were losing too much money. Many stations were closed and many train services were stopped. People had to find other means of transport.

In the 1950s and 1960s, fewer people travelled by train. Instead, people began to travel by car. Many new roads were built. Bypasses were built to take traffic away from busy town centres. Motorways were built to join large towns and cities. Britain's first motorway was the M1 between London and Birmingham, which was opened in 1959.

There are now almost 30 000 kilometres of motorway in Britain, and more are being built all the time. There are often traffic jams on motorways, especially because of roadworks or accidents.

**Source A**  *A traffic jam.*

However, trains still travelled between large towns and cities in Britain. In 1966, the first Intercity train was used, which could travel much more quickly than old steam or diesel trains. Many trains now run using electricity, which is much quieter and cleaner.

*Travelling by steam train.*

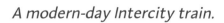

*A modern-day Intercity train.*

The first jet aeroplane to carry passengers was called the Comet. It began a regular passenger service in 1952. This was a small jet that could not carry many people. Since then passenger aeroplanes have become much larger. Modern jumbo jets can carry more than 500 people. New European planes can carry 800, though not yet in service.

The fastest passenger aeroplane in the world was Concorde. It was built by Britain and France and began flying in 1976. It flew at over 2000 kilometres per hour, but was taken out of service in 2004. Although modern aeroplanes like this are very fast, they are also very noisy, especially for people who live near large airports.

**Source B**  *A jumbo jet flying over some houses near an airport.*

## Road, rail and air

1. Why do many people travel by car today as opposed to rail? Give two reasons.
2. Why have more people started travelling by aeroplane since the 1950s?
3. What can cause a traffic jam on a motorway?
4. Describe how it feels to be stuck in a traffic jam like the one shown in **Source A**.
5. Imagine you live in one of the houses underneath the aeroplane in the photograph in **Source B**. Describe how the noise affects your life.

## Miles ahead

Think about how transport has changed in Britain since 1948.

1. Draw a chart to show the good and bad things about travelling by train, car and aeroplane.
2. Draw a time line to show how transport has changed in Britain since 1948.

## Key ideas

passenger aircraft

More and more people began to buy cars in the 1950s. One of the most famous cars of the time was the Morris Minor and later the Mini. The Mini was made by Austin and Morris and cost only £500.

**Source A** *A car assembly line today.*

Today, modern car factories use computers and robots to produce cars quickly and cheaply. This means that many factories can employ fewer staff.

**Source B** *A Morris Minor in 1949.*

**Source C** *A Mini in 1959.*

**Car crazy**

1. Find out what the differences are between car production in the 1940s and today? Use **Source A** to help you.
2. Look carefully at the pictures of the Morris Minor and the Mini (**Sources B** and **C**). How are these cars different from cars today? Are they similar?

Car manufacturers today bring out new models of car every few years, each one better than the last.

When people choose a new car they consider what it looks like, how fast it can go, and also how much fuel (diesel) it uses and how expensive it is to run. They also considered how safe they think the car is to drive.

Many people are also worried about how cars affect our environment, and so many cars use unleaded petrol. This helps to stop some poisonous gases escaping into the air.

**Life in the fast lane**

Find out more about cars in Britain since 1948.

1. Collect some photographs and advertisements of cars in the 1940s and 1950s, and for cars in the 1990s and present day. Make two displays to show how cars have changed.
2. Conduct a survey about cars. Ask five people about their cars – why they bought the car, what they like about it, and so on. Make a database of your findings.

# Car Crazy

**Source D**  *A car from the 1950s.*

**Source E**  *A car from 2006.*

## Changing cars

1. Look at the photographs of cars from the 1950s and the 2000s (**Sources D** and **E**). Write a list of three similarities and three differences between the cars.
2. Look at the chart of cars in Britain. How many cars were in Britain in 1950?

38

Car Travel

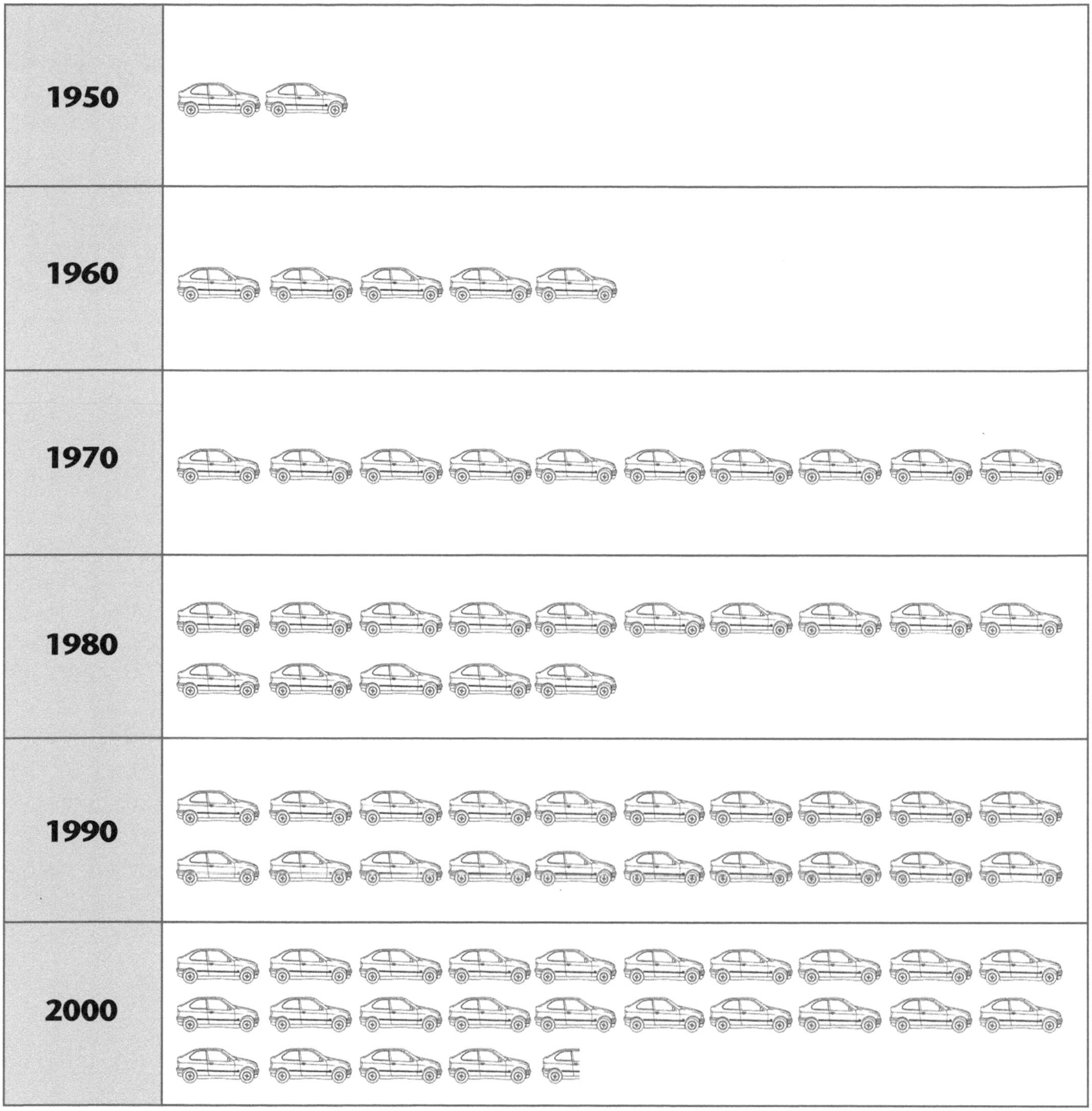

| | |
|---|---|
| **1950** | 🚗🚗 |
| **1960** | 🚗🚗🚗🚗🚗 |
| **1970** | 🚗🚗🚗🚗🚗🚗🚗🚗🚗🚗 |
| **1980** | 🚗🚗🚗🚗🚗🚗🚗🚗🚗🚗🚗🚗🚗🚗🚗 |
| **1990** | 🚗🚗🚗🚗🚗🚗🚗🚗🚗🚗🚗🚗🚗🚗🚗🚗🚗🚗🚗🚗 |
| **2000** | 🚗🚗🚗🚗🚗🚗🚗🚗🚗🚗🚗🚗🚗🚗🚗🚗🚗🚗🚗🚗🚗🚗🚗🚗🚗 |

*This chart shows the number of cars in Britain since 1950. Each car in the chart stands for a million cars on the roads.*

## Then and now

Draw and complete a chart like this to show the advantages and disadvantages of more cars in Britain.

| Advantages | Disadvantages |
|---|---|
| | |

Between 1948 and 1960, most of Britain's energy came from coal. It was used to heat homes, offices and schools. Coal was also used in power stations to make electricity, and as fuel for steam trains.

*A coal mine in Wales in the 1950s. South Wales was one of the largest coal mining areas in Britain. The area suffered much hardship and unemployment when many of the mines were closed in the 1960s, 1970s, 1980s and 1990s.*

In the 1940s and 1950s, there were hundreds of coal mines in Britain. Gradually, machines were introduced to do many of the jobs that had once been done by hand. This meant that during the 1960s and 1970s many miners were put out of work. The situation became worse in the 1970s when new sources of energy were found, such as oil and gas. In 1955, there were almost 900 coal mines in Britain, 40 years later there were fewer than 20 mines left.

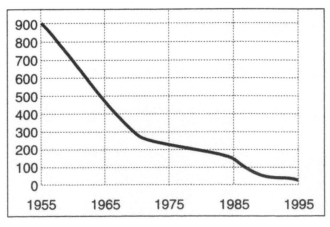

*This graph shows how the number of coal mines fell between 1955 and 1995.*

In the last 50 years there have been many changes in the way that Britain produces its energy. The first British nuclear power station was opened in the 1950s. In the 1960s and 1970s, alternative energy sources were discovered, including large reserves of oil and gas beneath the North Sea. Today we also have gas and oil fuel stations as well as hydro-electric power, which only represents a very small amount of Britain's energy. They are mainly found in the Scottish Glens, but only in areas which can cope with the effects.

*A wind farm is a very clean way of producing energy.*

*An oil rig in the North Sea, which is used to drill for oil and then pump it to the shore.*

Nuclear power stations have become unpopular because of the pollution they can cause. Many power stations that use coal, oil and gas also release large amounts of dirt and smoke into the environment.

Many people believe it is now very important to develop cleaner and more efficient ways of producing energy. One way of doing this is on a wind farm, which uses windmills to generate electricity. A wind farm in West Yorkshire has 23 windmills and could provide power for 4500 homes – the size of a small town.

## Power points

1. Describe the changes in the way Britain has produced its energy since 1948.
2. Why was the coal industry so important to Britain?
3. Give two reasons why many of Britain's coal mines closed between 1955 and the present day.
4. Write a list of the alternative ways of producing energy that are used in Britain today.

## Producing energy

Find out more about how energy has been produced in Britain.

1. What do the terms 'renewable' and 'non-renewable' mean?
2. Write a list of renewable and non-renewable energy sources. What are the advantages and disadvantages of each?

# (14) Pollution

**Source A** *Smog in London, 1952.*

**Source B** *The Braer oil disaster, 1993.*

Pollution can also happen at sea. In January 1993, an oil tanker called the Braer ran aground off the Shetland Islands. Oil leaked out of the tanker, and after six days an oil slick covered a large area of the sea. A large part of the coastline of Shetland was spoiled when oil was washed up.

Pollution has been a problem in Britain for many years. In 1952, thick smog (a mixture of smoke and fog) covered London for four days. The yellow smog was so thick that flares had to be carried in front of buses so that the drivers could see where they were going. The smog even got inside buildings, for example, cinemas had to close because people could not see the screen. The smog also made diseases like bronchitis much worse. Many people died.

## Dirty business

1. What is smog? Why did it kill some people in London in 1952?
2. Look at the photograph of the London smog (**Source A**). Describe what you think it would have been like to live in London at the time.
3. Describe what happened to the Braer oil tanker in 1993.
4. Look carefully at the photograph of the Braer disaster (**Source B**). What do you think made the oil spread so far?
5. What has happened in **Source D**?
6. Look at the list of facts. Write a list of ways in which these problems could be solved.
7. Design a poster like the anti-litter poster in **Source C**. Use the facts to help you.

In recent years, people have become worried about other types of pollution. Look at the facts.

**Source C** *An anti-litter poster.*

**Fact**

Radiation from a fire at the Windscale nuclear reactor in 1957 polluted areas of farmland. In April 1986, the Russian nuclear power station at Chernobyl exploded, sending a poisonous cloud over Britain and other countries. This caused pollution of farmland far away in Wales, northern England and Scotland.

**Fact**

In 1986, Britain released 3 760 000 tonnes of sulphur dioxide into the air from power stations. When mixed with moisture in the air it falls as acid rain. This damages lakes, forests and buildings.

**Source D** *Damage caused to a forest by acid rain.*

**Fact**

The build-up of gases in the atmosphere is helping to warm up the surface of the Earth. This is called the 'Greenhouse Effect'.

## Cleaning up

Find out more about pollution in Britain.

1. What did the government do to make sure that the London smog did not happen again?
2. Carry out an experiment with some oil and sand. Pour a small amount of oil into a tray of sand, and leave it for a few minutes. Describe carefully what has happened to the sand. What effect do you think 50 000 tonnes of oil would have on beaches and wildlife?

**Fact**

Gases called CFCs, which are pumped into the air from aerosols and refrigerators, are thought to be causing a hole in the ozone layer that protects us from the Sun's harmful rays. This can lead to serious diseases such as skin cancer.

## Key ideas

atmosphere          radiation
pollution

## Dirty Business

Pollution has been a problem in Britain for many years. It can have a terrible effect on the land, the air and the sea. One of the worst pollution disasters at sea was in 1993, when the Braer oil tanker hit rocks on the Shetland Islands. A large part of the coast of Shetland was polluted by oil.

3 January
*The oil tanker Braer left Norway, on a long journey to Canada.*

5 January, 2:30am
*The engine of the oil tanker stopped. It began drifting towards Shetland.*

5 January, 5:00am
*The coastguard was called.*

5 January, 7:00am
*A helicopter started taking the crew off the tanker.*

5 January, 9:40am
*A tug arrived and tried to pull the tanker away from Shetland. It failed.*

5 January, 11:20am
*The Braer hit rocks at Garths Ness in Shetland. Oil poured from the tanker.*

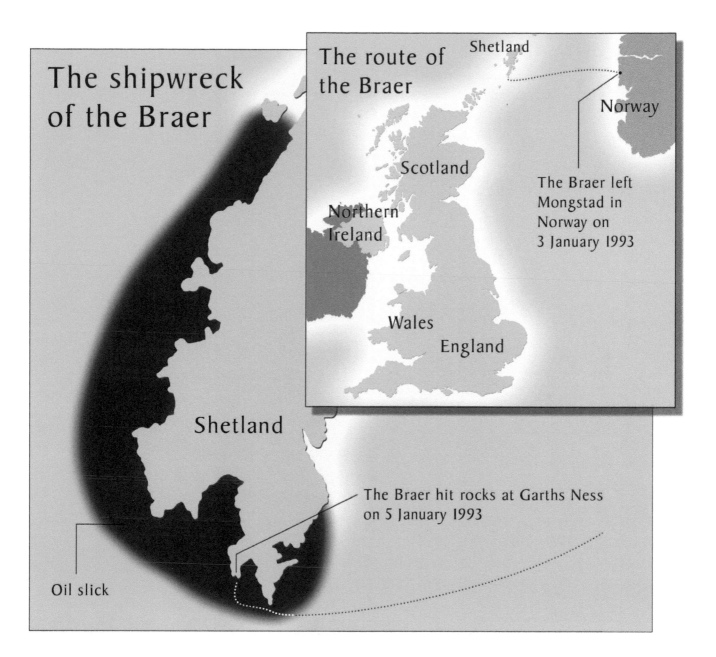

# The shipwreck of the Braer

**The route of the Braer**

Shetland

Norway

Scotland

Northern Ireland

Wales

England

The Braer left Mongstad in Norway on 3 January 1993

Shetland

The Braer hit rocks at Garths Ness on 5 January 1993

Oil slick

## Pollution

1. Using the information on these pages, explain what happened to the Braer.
2. Whose fault do you think the accident was?
3. Why do you think this?
4. What do you think could have been done to stop this accident happening?

## Oil slick

1. Choose one of the people from the following list. Imagine you were this person at the time of the Braer disaster. Write about what you did on that day and how you felt about it:
   - the captain of the Braer
   - the coastguard
   - an RSPCA officer
   - a person living on Shetland.
2. Find out about what happened to Shetland after the accident. Find out how the oil was cleaned up, how long it took and what the area looks like today.

Computers are part of everyday life in Britain. They are used for many things – to help us see distant stars, to stock supermarket shelves, to help fight disease, and to help us tell whether it will be sunny tomorrow. Computers can deal with information much faster than humans.

Charles Babbage invented the computer over 100 years ago. The first computers worked using cards with holes in them.

In the 1950s, new kinds of computers were built. They used small transistors instead of electric valves. This meant that computers were cheaper to make, could work faster, used less electricity and took up much less space.

**Source A**  *A computer in 1964.*

In the 1960s and 1970s, computers became cheaper and faster. The silicon chip was invented, which could hold the equivalent of thousands of transistors in a very small space. Silicon chips are very small and very thin, and meant that a new kind of computer could be made: the micro-computer.

*Computers are used in many ways at home.*

Micro-computers were made smaller and cheaper in the 1970s and 1980s. Many computers are now used in homes and offices. Silicon chips can be found in hundreds of things, such as toys, televisions and washing machines. Almost every part of life in Britain since 1948 and even before in the 1930s has been changed by computers.

**Source B**

## Changing computers

1. Who invented the first computer?
2. Explain how the invention of each of these things changed computers: the electric valve, the transistor, the silicon chip.
3. What happened to computers in the 1970s and 1980s? Why?
4. How is the computer in the photograph from the 1960s (**Source A**) different from the one in your classroom?
5. What are computers being used for in the photograph of the office (**Source B**)?

## Everyday life with computers

Think about how we use computers every day.

1. Carry out a survey at home or in school. Write a list of everyday things which use silicon chips. Use your information to make a computer database.
2. What do you think computers will be used for in the future?

## Key ideas

new technology

# Index